Extra MoJo! #2

the best of *MoJo!* 2013-2016

Edited by Mignon Ariel King

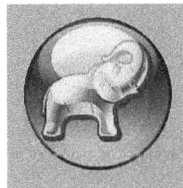

HIDDEN CHARM PRESS
New England, USA
2016

Extra MoJo! # 2: the best of *MoJo!* 2013-2016
©2016 Mignon Ariel King

Cover Art: "Maya" photograph © 2015 Patricia Wallace Jones

HIDDEN CHARM PRESS
NEW ENGLAND, USA

http://hiddencharmpress.wordpress.com
mojo_hcp@outlook.com

ISBN#: 9780692768464

This collection is dedicated to the late Marcie Eanes.
We who knew her, whether in person or via social media,
miss her smile, sense of humor, and sweet spirit.
Rest in peace, Sister.

EDITOR'S INTRO

Even most bookworms are social beings on some level. We seek out celebrations, teamwork, and traditions that keep us together – individually and socially. Congratulations, world, for every family member, friend, respected neighbor, or enjoyed colleague who helps you feel connected. I hope you enjoy the words of our diverse yet connected community of Black women writers!

Mignon Ariel King
Editor and Publisher
Boston, Massachusetts
Autumn, 2016

MARCIE EANES was a poet and journalist who explored love and life to the fullest. She is the author of *Sensual Sounds*, and *Passion's Zest*. *Cameo*, her memoir, describes her reinvention from newspaper reporter to traveling poet after surviving a near-fatal car accident at age 23. Her poetry has been published in numerous anthologies including *di-verse-city*, the official anthology of the Austin International Poetry Festival 2011-2014. Her writings also appeared in *Essence* and *Seventeen* magazines. A graduate of Marquette University, she lived in Racine, WI.

Ode to Joy

Ode to joy found in life.
Breath in lungs, eyes to see.
Other senses taken for granted
 are the very gifts
  Thanksgiving means.

Ode to joy for special talents.
Blessings not meant to be wasted.
Unique in design, waiting for expression.
 Peace in soul is found when they are shared.
  Ode to family and friends.

Riches more precious than coins.
Comfort, guides, sister, brother;
human love is the soul's elixir
 for what ails
  time after time

Ode to love in all its forms.
Four-legged is family too!
Holding us close in love
 with loyalty, trust and more.
  The only charge is to treat them well
   and respectfully every day.

Unheard Screams

She wakes up screaming
every morning.
All hear her angry roar
through thin apartment walls.
Easy to spot without voice,
baby on hip, two clinging
to each leg.
All three under six years.
Barely 22 years on Earth herself,

she's exhausted beyond age.
Her mama died at the hands
of her dad.
All alone since age eight.
Sex had so many meanings
other than intimate attraction,
sometimes only a mere exchange.
Many promises
made without clothes.
Few came true
when daddies disappeared.
Seeds made her
too sick to please or barter.

Telling neighbors
she don't need handouts
after throwing latest aid letter
on the ground;
they don't know
how deeply rejections hurt.
Latest was for a job
which held promises
for better.
Food stamps cuts
go into effect
next week.
A smart student with good grades
once upon a time,
endless demands leave
little time for much needed sleep.

Friends joke and tease
until temper calms down,
not stopping until they hear laughs.
They sit on stoop, enjoy summer day,

kids playing games, barbecue's tasty.

Groovin' music brings
everyone together.
Shooters' guns blast
outdoor peace.
All wildly scream and scatter,
hoping no one dies at the scene.
She searches and yells
for her babies
while running for cover.

Clutching each close.
Girl child bolts
into her apartment.
Four duck down,
scream loudly
behind closed door,
tears drenching all.
No answers to solve
this unending nightmare.
Reporters tell stories
then fade.
She and three sinking deeper
into poverty's widening canyon.
Frustrated with social programs,
waking up daily
to unyielding fear.

Selfies

She studies her nude body
by taking selfies,
posing in mirrors,
and snapping frames of jiggly bits

hiding underneath
clothes,
sheets,
in darkness.
Her greatest challenge
is to love
herself
Now.
Not waiting for lover's approval
after losing ten pounds
or health fails....
Selfies push past barriers
to shatter destructive thoughts looping
inside her head all waking hours,
repeating she's not
beautiful
desirable
sensual past a certain age.

Seasoned woman staring back
in mirror has lived
full-bodied,
without restraint.
Her survival is crucial
for the younger generation.
A sturdy example of a female
who speaks in bold tones,
not a timid voice
afraid of separate.
And attempting to silence
uninhibited yell
gathering steam deep down in root
is the same one
who once believed best days
were over   7

because all seemed sweeter
when she was a younger self.

Confidence rules life now.
Head held high, insecurity gone.
Selfies reflect peace
inside soul,
lighter spirit, playful times.
She shapes her world
the ways she pleases,
learning the simple word 'no'
preserves, not kills.
Her newly found freedom
attracts richer meaning.
Being fulfilled
assures love, not hurt.
Younger women
ask questions,
follow her examples
intently studying
every move.
Breathtaking feminine energy
takes new root.

Performer's Support

She pursues passion for two.
Stage spotlight shines brightly,
casting shimmering glow.
Her energy is supernatural,
magnetic for all to see.
Everyone wants to touch her,
see her, be her,
always clamor for more
every time she seduces

in that single spotlight.

Her number one fan waits offstage.
Alone, in the wings,
he knows her act.
Understanding intimately
why she's drawn to this life,
he beams and smiles broadly
despite being mistaken for the help.
His babe glows inside out.
Stage life makes him

love her more.

--Marcie Eanes

From *Passion's Zest - a collection* (Transcendent Zero Press, 2013)

**

My Journey In Becoming A Writer
By Cherrell Bates

Being a teenager is all about finding out who you are and where you want to go in life. I was no different. I spent those years trying to decide whether I wanted to be a teacher, work in advertising or become a fashion buyer. I ultimately decided that I wanted to be a fashion buyer; so I went to college, majored in marketing, grabbed a BBA, yet today I work in the medical field. My passion for buying quickly evaporated, but one passion of mine remained true and that was writing.

I have been writing since I was fourteen years old in the eighth grade. I wrote about silly crushes and teenage fantasies that involved first kisses, first dates and going to prom. This began my love affair with romance. I spent hours imagining falling in love and happy endings. I would create hundreds of complicated characters in my head. I could be in school, riding in a car or sitting in the middle of church service. It didn't matter where I was, my mind was always racing.

Still, despite my desire to always write, I never imagined becoming an author. I never considered publishing anything that I wrote. I thought that was for the extremely talented and prominent, such as Zane, Mary B. Morrison, E. Lynn Harris or the late Maya Angelou. I had no clue in how to start a career in writing.

Yet, throughout my twenties, I kept writing. Those short stories, turned into novels. Before I knew it, I had written four of them. With the exception of a couple of paragraphs here or there, no one ever read my work. I kept these stories of heartbreak, betrayal and passion to myself. I wasn't confident enough in myself or in my writing to allow someone into this imaginative world that had been a part of my life since I was a teenager.

Everyone knew I was a writer, though. Without reading my words, they encouraged me. "Why don't you publish your books?" If it wasn't my mother, it was my college roommate, one of my best friends or my boyfriend. Eventually, I was asking myself the same thing, "Why aren't you publishing your books?"

I grew excited at the possibility of seeing my work sitting on the shelf of a big chain bookstore, but so many doubts were holding me back. How do I begin? How do I contact a literary agent? Do I need a literary agent? How do I get in contact with a publishing house?

I began to take publishing a book seriously. I researched the steps I needed to make my dream a reality. I ultimately decided to self-publish. I decided that it will allow me the freedom to do things my way.

I knew this was what I wanted to do, but the years started to creep by. Every New Years, I would lift my glass, telling my friends, "This is the year." The book was written; I just had to get it out there. I had to put in the work to accomplish my goals and stop procrastinating.

It took me being laid off to make it happen. I sat at home for months, staring at walls, watching daytime talk shows and applying for jobs. I was bored. I felt lost. I was unmotivated.

Finally, I asked myself, "What are you doing? Why are you sitting here?" I grabbed my notebook and I sat in front of the computer and I began to type. Before I knew it, I was finished. I could finally see this happening for myself. I was going to publish a book.

Everything fell into place after that. I had my book cover. I had my editor.

I had my account with a print on demand printing company. I was ready. There was nothing left to stop me.

So in April of 2014, I submitted my book. The very next day, I was ordering my proof. When I received that proof in the mail, it was an amazing feeling. I had imagined seeing my words in print, but actually seeing it was ten times more rewarding.

April 29, 2014, my first published novel, "Yield Not To Temptation", went live on Amazon. I was officially a published author. People could buy my book. They could download my e-book. They could read the words that I had been hiding for years.

I didn't have this big marketing budget. Social Media became my best friend. I pushed my book daily. I sent emails, page invites, messages, and shared countless links. I encouraged people to review my work, invite their friends to like my page, to share my links and to just spread the word. There is nothing like word of mouth.

It's been a year; I haven't become a well-known author. I didn't sell thousands of books. At this point, I can't even consider writing a part time job. I didn't make a bunch of money. That's all okay, though.

I did something that I always wanted to do. In all of these years that I could never imagine being a published author, deep down, that's what I wanted to be. In a very disappointing period in my life, I achieved that. My name in pink shiny letters, sprawled across a book. My book.

I wrote this story about love, betrayal, forgiveness and finding your way. I wrote about flawed and complicated characters, making bad choices. I intertwined very human behavior with scripture. I wanted this story to reflect that it doesn't matter how many mistakes you make, God will never leave you. He will always guide you.

I am working on my next novel, which will be out by summer 2015. Then I will work on the sequel to my first novel. As long as my mind continues to race and my creative juices continue to flow, I will keep writing.

This is just the beginning. I want to do this for the rest of my life. I may not make a lot of money or become a prominent author, but I will have a rewarding career as an author. To hear someone who has read my book, telling me, "I loved this book," is all the reward I will ever need.

**

Just Breathe

It begins with space-freedom.
Moves beyond explanations, and refuses mere definitions,
Created from hollowed words and empty sounds
Strung across nothing
Only to fall then crash.
The echo speaks,
Just breathe.
Open to the possibilities
Breathe.
Explore all your soul sings.
Lift up, ever beyond that space.
It belongs to you
This piece of blank-waiting.
And yet the moment will pass.
Hush.
Be still-just breathe.
Hush.
Can you hear it?
The pieces of your life
Falling like a quiet snow, gently caressing the ground.
Breathe.
Be still.
Watch your spirit move
Hush.
Long enough to touch.
Just breathe.
Can you hear your name?
Above the whispered rush of ordinary.
Spirit and soul
Life itself dancing
Released from its frame.
Do you hear it? Beneath the pounding hustle of days
That space where something should have been
Life laughing,
Hush.
Just breathe.

--Anna K. Betts   14

Atlas Brown was born in Fort Worth, Texas. She is a graduate of the University of North Texas with a Master's in Library Science; holds a B.A. in English-Creative Writing with a minor in African-American Studies (from the University of Houston. Additionally, Keeton is a Fellow of the UNT Graduate Student Teaching Excellence Program, a member of Beta Phi Mu International Library & Information Studies Honor Society, and is a member of the Honors College.

As a Change-Agent, Keeton is the creative director and publisher of ART | library deco, an online African American art journal.

Currently, Brown is working on her first book of essays and a digitization project. The writer is an avid blogger who publishes monthly posts about her experiences as an early career librarian. In addition, she is the Founder of *Black Women Intelligentsia* (BWI), a virtual Wikipedia Edit-Thon Group documenting the lives of African American historical figures from the past. The creative guru is an Academic Librarian and Assistant Professor of Library Science at Lincoln University in Jefferson City, MO.

blue. blue. blues.

Pick up yo' bags lil' gal and move on
ain't nothing wrong
blue. blue. blues.
Life is what you make it   15

That's what dey' says
cause U iz tru to what's new
blue. blue. blues.
Rain, Snow, Hail, Wind
can't stop Yo' unique trendz
"Oh some people tell me the worried blues ain't bad"
blue. blue. blues.
yeah, he left you in yo' tracks
But, you got yo' steps right back
Smile, honey chile!
Command the earth to shake
Rattle
Roll
Shake yo' ass
Put dem' heels on
and stroll...
Pick up yo' bags lil' gal and move on
ain't nothing wrong
blue. blue. blues
dah keyz to life
are in Ur dreams
get that suitcase togetha
U can n'dure in any type of wea'tha
blue. blue. blues.
"Oh some people tell me the worried blues ain't bad"
Cauzzzzzzzzzzzzzzzzzzzzzzzzzzzzz
Everythang
iz
allllllllllllllllllllllllllllllllllllllllllllllllllright
blue. blue. blues.

--*Atlas Brown*

**

16

Rekaya Gibson, Food Blogger and Recipe Developer of *The Food Temptress*, is the author of three novels and two children's books. Her latest cookbook, *Cooking on a Dollar Store Budget*, reflects her love of food. She has written for several publications including *Writer's Digest Books*, *Cabo Living Magazine*, and *Lake of the Ozarks Second Home Living Magazine*. Currently, she reviews cookbooks for *Cuisine Noir Magazine* and travel articles for Amtrak's microsite.

Ms. Gibson owns and operates Gibson Girl Publishing Company, LLC, and she loves being a professional aunt.

Unequal Among Women
By Rekaya Gibson

Last year, my brother-in-law posted a picture of my niece and nephew on Facebook, mainly to show their mom, who had been stationed at a military base in Qatar. They were having so much fun. AvaRose was at home sitting in her high chair while her four-year-old brother fed her. She hadn't quite turned two years old yet. I could see her smile beneath her oatmeal face, soiled clothes, and of course the messy floor. Most people left pleasant comments underneath the image; however, a few women left – what I thought were – insensitive statements about AvaRose's hair. She had an end-of-the-day wild afro. Her hair reminded me of Beyonce and Jay-Z's daughter, Blue Ivy, which by the way, was around the same time a petition was circulating to make Beyoncé comb her daughter's hair.

My sister felt bad that folks were talking about her baby's hair. She called her husband had him remove the photo. He complied with her wishes, but it brings up the question, why would something as miniscule as a child's hair disturb people to the point where they felt the need to say something negative? I also wondered what AvaRose's life would be like growing up in America if she was already experiencing criticism about her locs. I thought the photograph was adorable, one of the few times the parents will get to capture their children's brother-sisterly love on public display.

Months later, another woman — a family member — said AvaRose was fat. My reply was, "No, she is not!" She was barely a toddler; she had just turned two a couple a weeks prior. Once I said that, the woman justified her answer by comparing AvaRose's size to another two-year old boy who was at the party. My thought was, Why does this matter?

I wondered what else was in store for AvaRose? She has milk-chocolate skin. I cannot imagine how she will be judged compared to others with lighter skin. She is a fun, loving girl who enjoys participating in pronto dance parties. What if she wants to be like her mom who used to groove without reserve to Olivia Newton-John's, *Let's Get Physical?* Will AvaRose be considered a hoochie for shaking her body? I love the way AvaRose commands the room. If she keeps this trait, will she be considered stuck up? When she asks for what she wants, for instance, playing with her favorite pink pig, will she be considered a bitch? Heaven forbid if she joins the debate team in high school. Will she be labeled an angry black female?

My wish is that she will be allowed to enjoy cupcakes like she did at her brother's birthday party without someone thinking she's had enough because of the white frosting stuck to her face. When she goes off to college, I'm hoping she takes after my love of math, reading, and writing.

If so, I hope no one calls her a nerd. When she speaks well, I pray no one will say she talks 'white.' I can already hear myself scream, "Go 'head, girl," as she becomes a leader and an independent thinker in total control of her own destiny. Perhaps, she will join the military and fight for peace and freedom along with other service members, making America proud.

As women continue to fight for equality among men, we also have to stamp out the belittling of women, youth, and children. I will have to teach AvaRose to find and surround herself with a diverse group of people who exude compassion, confidence, and intelligence. Also, to gravitate toward those whose perspectives don't contaminate her sense of wonder and view of the world. Many great women exist on this earth who support and respect one another. My wish is that she gets the opportunity to know and interact with them. I hope that whatever AvaRose decides to do with her life, she knows that she is beautiful, smart, and most importantly, she is loved.

**

Mignon Ariel King is a third-generation New Englander who was born in Boston City Hospital and has never lived outside of Massachusetts. Her father's parents were English teachers; her mother was a pre-K reading specialist. Ms. King, an alumna of Simmons College for Women, holds a Master of Arts in English degree and identifies as a womanist. She taught college-level English for a decade or so. She was a featured poet 24 times from 2009-2011 and could often be heard singing Hard Rock tunes from the '70s, frequently while wearing cowboy boots even in the snow.

Four parts of King's multi-genre autobiographical pentalogy (memoir, poetry trilogy, novella) have been published by Hidden Charm Press, ALL-CAPS Publishing, and Tell-Tale Chapbooks. For more info, see the blog *Making Books* at mignonarielking.wordpress.com and the Hidden Charm Press and Tell-Tale Chapbooks websites or Facebook pages.

Ommminous Boston Nights

What would you do if I sang out of tune?
-- Would you stand up and walk out on me?
Lend me your ears and I'll sing you a song.
-- I will try not to sing out of key. *

If you lie in the dark, quiet room long enough,
you'll find a sun of your own. Perhaps it starts
out small, yellowing sepia, so dim you might

think your eyes are playing merry with you.
There are little memories that will begin to tug
at the corners of your mind: times on Mass Ave

eating dates all night with other bachelor-girls,
spreading pate and toasting with wine all
the boys you'd ever loved, mostly just cheering

a newbie's one-bedroom condo, right after her
very bad divorce. But then comes the disquiet
of music, the sacred syllables that know you,

engorging your sun to blue. *I get by with a little help
from my friends.* You even surprised yourself then
with a lively retell of Brighton's sex against the wall

with a stoned guitarist, the dining room so black
you could not find words to shoo away a roommate
who actually stepped through the doorway a few

feet away, face larger and paler in lightlessness
as she peered around, thank God without flicking on
the light-switch. Now you can also laugh about the night

someone was downstairs in the huge old house near
Andrew Station, Sherry's boyfriend running into the hall
with a rope ladder, motioning toward the attic window.

You, instead, wielded a field hockey stick, rushing down
the stairs at the intruder -- *Ha!!! The* early-returning roomie
screamed for her life. -- *Hey, goomba, next time call before*

before slipping the chain lock at 4 am in Dorchester!
Pressed now against your soul-musician on the worst
night of your life, eyes closed on the dance floor, sun

and moon phases are merged by the mahogany saxophonist,
and your orange sphere glows timeless as you become
immortally in friendship and in love.

Oh, I get by with a little help from my friends. Ooh!
*I get high with a little help from my friends!**

[*Song lyrics by John Lennon and Paul McCartney]

Stepping

i.
We'll walk through the Old South End area, where July 4th
is months in the past...or the future...yet the city feels sieged.
Out-of-towners (snared by the romance of lobster in Boston,

a city steeped in tea party history and wimpled witches now
martyred, statuesqued, near the State House) keep coming
even in the snow. They litter Harvard Square, hoping to see

Damon or Affleck settings or to taste the hasty pudding that,
amusingly enough, requires hours and hours of strong stirring .
I wouldn't mind so much if only the bulbs would stop flashing

as I sail trainbound over the Charles River, fishing for pithy
when all my besotted brain wants to do is write about love.

ii.

In the years '48 to '49 two Boston sweethearts were only dating
until she was 21ish so they could run off to get hitched, back
North where they had originally come from two separate poles,

"upper" versus "cow" Hampshire. In one small area of Boston
my parents had finally been able to sit at the same table to eat
or to touch two pairs of hands to two waists or sets of shoulders.

Nobody at Wally's or the Top Hat gave a hoot what hue true
music and soul food fans were. My fair mother was Black too,
but when stupid people make quick assumptions, they stick.

Yet, here I was in 2013, stepping onto Columbus Avenue, out
into the only-an-inch perfection of snow to go hear children
singing, singing for MLK, singing for unity, singing for love.

iii.

Tall and tan and accustomed to eyes rolling, rude lips pursing,
questions and challenges to my very being, I felt no glares.
I happen to like cowboy boots with a skirt. Operatic voices

rang in the school my mother attended before they eloped.
So I thought while we walked: this is where my parents
fell in love with each other's voice, smiled for the first time

at each other's eyes. Around the corner is where the only
photograph I've seen of them, paired as they were for life,
was recorded on film. I see that scalloped photo, their pact,

followed by two Kodak generations of tipped mortar boards.
Love isn't about making babies. It's about changing minds.

--Mignon Ariel King

[Both poems are from the work-in-progress *Words of Flight: poems of tribute 3*]

**

Meredith King is a creative generalist, writer, visual and performing artist. She currently resides in Cleveland, OH and is passionate about using the arts in innovative ways to transform individuals and strengthen communities.

I Need A Poem

I need a poem
cause I feel
so much that I can't say
that it takes
rice pudding and French fries
to keep me from
exploding

I need a poem
cause there's a chick I barely know
and hardly like
crying on my shoulder
like I'm her sister
in misery
when she's happy
she doesn't speak to me at all

I need a poem
cause I need patience
for those whose good intentions
disregard who I am
and still manage
to offend me

I need a poem
cause I have a headache
in two separate worlds
there's a swarm of locusts
inside my head
frenzy
dissipating only as a hammer
strikes my temple
every five minutes

I need a poem
cause somewhere along the line
I changed
from floating
in healthy isolation
to drowning
in social anxiety
and panic

I need a poem
cause an invitation to a birthday celebration
made my hands
shake today
and that made me scared
and wonder how long I'd be here
I didn't used to do that
I don't want to turn another year
in silence

Give me a poem
to speak what I cannot say

words that warm where there is cold
and love where there is
empty
Give me a poem

to hold my hand cause I can't see anything but water
and I'm scared
I'll fall
it's deeper than it seems
and there's nothing
and no one
to keep me from sinking

Give me a poem
to belt at the top of my lungs
one that won't laugh when my voice cracks
it'll just be glad
I still know how to sing
sometimes
it's hard to breathe in the silence
that's why I need a poem
to be my voice
and my air

Belief

I remember taking a chance
going to sleep with love in my ears
I remember
wanting and needing
slipping
falling
and then breaking
into pieces too sharp to count

I believed in possibility and future
in souls and soulmates
I believed in rainy days and sweaty bodies
fertilized eggs and promises

made before God and the Federation
I believed in want satisfied and needs fulfilled
and dreams too big to defer
but the past tense is the landlord that throws you out on the street
when the present can't pay the rent
and my belief was the 10 year old
who sees mama putting the presents under the tree in the middle of the night
and realizes Santa ain't real
cause unless you live on 34th Street and God sends you a miracle
the belief ain't coming back
and when you meet that bearded white man
that shows you the meaning of Christmas and life
you're grateful
but he ain't the Santa you left cookies for at age 5
or the Santa that got you a brand new ten-speed at 9
even though money was tight
he's the Santa that brings tube socks and ties
sweaters and small household appliances
the Santa who gives gifts with predetermined spending amounts
to keep the emotions under control
he's the Santa you need to get through the holidays,
but not the one that makes you happy
he's the Santa that lets you breathe
but not the one that made the midnight air taste like ice cream

I'm too old for Santas
but I still believe
I believe in passion
in souls
in knowing and discovering
I believe in want and need
in beauty and power
negotiated
not taken
I believe in gametes and kept promises
in ignoring the statistics
and being vulnerable anyway
I believe in saying what you mean and meaning what you say

and going after what you want
even if
it doesn't want you
I believe in peace
and most of all
I believe that my heart has just enough to space
to love the way I look in someone else's eyes

But there's no miracles on my street
and I'll never believe the same way
again

Letter to a Stranger

You were wearing a blue shirt
with the buttons in all the wrong holes
and me
a half-naked figure
huddled
at the corner of the bed
I couldn't stop watching you
Fire and brimstone in the contraction of every muscle
rage unseen
destroying everything in sight
including you and me

That was the day

Long before the first bruise
the first excuse
and the first apology
Before fists met faces
and passion met fear
trapped in a dangerous dance
somewhere
between devotion and terror
muscles tensed, teeth grinding, footsteps heavy
and me

huddled
and confused and frightened
knowing something had ended
and something else begun
hands left trembling, fears left unleashed
words left unspoken
You never left but walked away just the same

That was the day
Your touch became foreign
your movements mechanical
your eyes far away
I wanted to take that moment and freeze it
fix it
tame the creature that consumed your insides
and put your heart back in my reach
grab you in my arms
and sing you to sleep

but I couldn't

And that was the day we became strangers

**

Briefly, a little about the author – me! My name is **Diane L. Lewis** and I am the Arts Council of Indianapolis' 2010 Robert D. Beckmann Emerging Artist Fellow. The Beckmann Fellowship has provided me the opportunity to develop as a writer, with the goal of producing a full-length book of poetry. Most recently I have been able to publish my work in *Tall Grass Writer's Guild Anthology 2013 & 2014,* (Outrider Press), *Reckless Writing Poetry Anthology 2013*, (Chatterhouse Press), and in *Flying Island Literary Journal* (2014). I am a member of Famous Writers Club and the Indiana Writer's Center.

Women

there are high heel women
and low-slung pump wearing women
and flat shoe, boot strappin' women
flip-flop rather be barefoot women

plain cup-o-joe women

double half, decaf latte with foam women
i only drink herbal tea women
folgers instant on-the-run women

let's go out to eat in a fancy restaurant women
do you want cornbread with your black eyed peas? women
grab some KFC on the way home, honey women
baby, why don't you cook tonight? women

run my fingers through my hair women
time to get a perm women
wouldn't trade my locks for nothing women
live under a dryer at the beauty parlor women

fiesty firey women
demur diva women
crafty suspicious women
devoted God-fearing women

they are our mothers, our grannies, our aunties
our girlfriends, our sisters, yes even our daughters
they go to movies, church, weddings, graduations
they are chocolate, molasses, vanilla, honey and cinnamon
some are tall, others not so
others are wide, some not so
and they are all special to me
they are how i know

i am loved

Velvet's Dignity

Velvet is not a tragic victim of circumstances,
Velvet is not a statistic,
she has no label or operating instructions,
only an expiration date

blessed by her Creator
she will
fulfill her purpose, complete her destiny,
find passion, discover love

Velvet is daughter, mother, sister, comrade,
revolution to others who struggle

she is in no particular order
on any given day
writer, poet, thinker, artist

her dress is torn, her hair disheveled,
her pockets empty
she is abused, mistreated, neglected, forlorn, forgotten

invisible

Velvet sleeps each night under the railroad tracks
Velvet dances barefoot under the stars
the music is in her head
Velvet has dignity

Velvet is not a tragic victim of circumstances
her brilliant mind wastes away on the mundane
the mediocre
dried out eyes
watch for a sign of rain...

Taraja (Hope)

while caught in cross-town traffic
she strains, water breaking forth
laboring
to bring an unborn poem into the world
to defy abortive defeat
amongst exhaust, smoke, fumes
and flying hubcaps

thrust

a tiny miracle
this pregnant poet tenaciously births Hope

takes her first breath
sees the first light of day
small, underweight
with 20 lines
2 stanzas, no rhythm
perfect
beautiful

push

Hope's first breath ends in a cry
the days' journal entry absorbs the amniotic flow
of another masterpiece
i think i will name this baby
Taraja
for she is my hope

--*Diane L. Lewis*

**

Lynda McLellan is a graduate of California State Polytechnic University, Pomona (Cal Poly Pomona) where she studied English. While in school, she assisted one of her professors by researching and compiling poetry for an anthology, and so was introduced to a larger world of poetry-- particularly modern female poets from around the world. Upon deeper reflection over the years, Lynda has come to see poetry as not just a collection of pretty words, but as tools to paint pictures of life. She is currently working on a collection of poems on the subject of poverty.

The Cupboard

The woman who reached in the cupbord and found nothing in her hand
there was no wine, no fruit, no meat and no bread
she filled her head with longing for days that were plentiful in every need
The woman lifted her eyes, her hands, and her heart, as she got down on her knees
Every night she wept and prayed and found to much avail
life was an empty, hopeless, frightening journey
not knowing what was ahead.
But every day
she found a crumb when she was out in the field
a morsel among the townsmen

a bite while wandering streets long and thin
her feet were bare
she had nothing to give
and all she could do was take
receive from her God, His mercy
left a trail of crumbs in his wake
And one day the woman's path went to heaven's gates
and she ate for the first time as much as she wanted was baked
she ate bread til she was full, water to quench her thirst
and all that she had ever wanted or needed she found
For the Lord, without her asking the question the question in her mind,
"You went without, so you when you got here, you'd realize what you'd found."

Women's Souls

Is there ever a time when women divide
love from life
joy from necessity
we nurture these
we need these
we birth the increase
in other people's lives
we are made whole
even when faced with strife
we are stronger than men
stronger than steel
stronger than bone
indestructible life force
from soul and blood and marrow
women are solid
like a forest of old trees
they stand together
so the wind ruffles only the their topmost leaves
tall and majestic
even when they're short
there is something in them
that others know nothing of

we are a resiliant sort
we fill churches
we fill homes
we feel glorious things
all at the hand of life's strings
we play like a harp
in the rain
dashing, singing, dancing
love is in our hearts
our minds
our spirits
the very blood that courses through our vains
has a river of gold with in it

--Lynda McLellan

**

April Vanesha Parker says: "I have been writing since the age of sixteen. I would like to inspire others to want to write as a healthy way to express themselves."

The Road to Serenity
By April V. Parker

The day I knew that I wanted to be a singer was the day I discovered a cassette tape of Whitney Houston's debut album. I was about six or seven years old. I also knew that I wanted to be on television. I do not remember what show or event inspired me. All that I know is that I wanted to be on television. I did not discover acting until I was in high school. Once I started performing, I knew that I wanted to continue doing it. An event from my childhood that stands out is the death of my biological mother from breast cancer when I was six years old. I do not remember any other significant occurrence other than that as a child.

When I was in high school, I performed in my first play *And Then There Was* None. I played Presley York, a singer. I also did a pageant. For the talent portion of the pageant I performed a poem that I wrote called "Hero": Someone told me what I couldn't do, where I couldn't go, who I couldn't be/that's when I decided that my next hero would be me." I also sang Mariah Carey's "Hero." I won the crown and the trophy for "Most Talented." I experience.

I was born three months premature, so I had to stay in the hospital for three months. The hospital staff thought that I was going to die because I only weighed two pounds. But I am a fighter. I have a warrior spirit. I know why I finally made the decision to follow my dreams. I have always loved performing. I am going to write this memoir in hopes that some woman or man will be inspired to follow their dreams. If I can just do that, I will be satisfied.

When I was a little girl singing in choirs, I never wanted to sing a solo because I did not want the attention solely on me. I only sang duets. One time, as I sang my part of "O Happy Day," I started thinking that if only my biological mother could have been alive and there in the audience to hear me sing...and tears started running down my face. But I kept on singing. Now, I do not mind singing solo. Singing lifts my spirit and brings me joy, peace, and happiness. Having a strong spiritual connection with God allows me to totally experience life without being concerned with the uncertainty of the future. Singing was my road to serenity.

**

Helen Patmon has had her plays performed in the Boston area. She has an MFA in theatre from the University of Oklahoma and a M.Ed. from Lesley University.

Kissing the Blue

Louis was born anemic,
so Mama fed him ice cream.

I dreamed of lapping ice cream,
the rap-tap of eggs, the blop of butter,
the whoosh of sugar swirling and twirlings,
as Mama made that bowl sing a sweet low purrr.

Louis always got an extra dollop because,
he was anemic, even after he wasn't anemic anymore.
Baby Sister chirped behind him,
so he was crowned, "Fearless Leader."

Fearless Leader took it into his head to fly.
He believed in flying.
He tied a rope to a brick,
and the other to a cat's tail,

39

heaved that screeching, squalling creature
into the air and over the roof,
"He's flying! He's flying!" he surmised.

With Baby Sister in hand, Fearless Leader
scampered up to the highest branches of a fat cottonwood tree,
took out Mama's pink umbrella and jumped.
Umbrella floomphed and bomp! to the ground they went.
Dusting himself off he declared,
"We can fly."

With capes and robes, all sorts of paper airplanes,
Fearless Leader honed his fling skills.

Then one morning, he rose, put on his shoes, and set out for school.
                                    "Today I shall fly."

A giant saw horse stood before him,
the clank of steel shifted in the air,
as steel chains like a little girl's long braid intertwined.
Fearless Leader silenced the clink to a clank,
put his hand on the braid with a clunk,
then sat on that wooden barrette like a throne.
He planted his feet flat on the sand and began his ascent.
Step, step backwards, tips of toes remain in the sand,
Release, legs pop out straight ahead.
Again and again, thrusting and folding, thrusting and folding, until wind
whizzed by his side.
Higher and higher pumping and thrusting to kiss the blue.

Looking up he seemed so small.

Fearless Leader did what he wanted to do.
He said it, so he had to do it.
One foot at a time,
He grasp the steel chain braids,
stood high and tall.

Then he jumped. For a moment...he flew.

40

He also broke his arm.

As I sit beneath a big cottonwood,
holding a stick in my hand,
drawing everything but nothing in particular,
with endless blue above me,
I wonder what happens to flying when one grows old.

Priority Mail

"Priority Mail" cube perched on my back porch,
Writing crooks and turns in my name and I remember you,
No postmark needed, I see "Oklahoma" and I remember you.
No return address needed I know you and me,

I never thought we looked the same,
but everybody called me, you and you, me,
even Mama sometimes.

I remember you little and me big,
"Stay outtah that dirt gurl!"

I was your keeper.

Mama sealed that deal with Switch.

I was your keeper.

Last time I saw you we only whispered,
Not a kind word between us.
What was there to say? Mama was gone.
"We don't haftah behave."

I see you perched, sitting on my back steps,
with amber light streaming across your face,
fumbling keys trying to fit in slots, never ever to easily click,
"Do you have problems with your hands crampin'? They say it's arthritis.

Mama had it."

Fear of you will not let me breathe.
Click, door opens, I walk right in.
Climb far too many steps at the end of the day, and I remember you.
"Who taught you to cook them sausages and cabbage, tender and almost limp?
Shouldah been me."

I remember you sitting too close beside me, last time I saw you,
"Doctah say such thang as a broken heart syndrome that'll killyah."
Should I remember you,
                    perched at my back door,
                    beat feet down steps,
                    pick you up and hold you tight,
                    be your keeper,
forgetting unanswered phone calls,
letters never sent,
wanting to be with you
I venture death and call your name.

--Helen Patmon

**

Brittany Rogers happily juggles the roles of mother, wife, poet, educator, and mentor on a daily basis. Brittany is currently a member of the Freshwater WordSmith Slam team, which will be competing at the National Poetry Slam in August 2016. She has poetry forthcoming in *Eunoia Review*.

Lying to my Daughter About Why Her Biological Father and I Got Divorced.

euphemisms taste like: the last supper-
enough flavor to soak your teeth. so
dry you are bound to choke.
Bones singing with pain;
you needed "he wasn't the best dad"
more than I needed to be brutally honest.

he possessed more personalities than
I had shoes;-
1 drunk, 1 snake charmer; 1
fallen wire during a thunderstorm;

1 who hits pregnant woman across face
when she tries to rescue him from the rotting
skull of his idolatry.

You, daughter have always been more
emotion than my palms can comfortably
cradle, more glasses shattering
than tucking a pout in the bitter of your lip.

I tell myself there is none of his
crooked in your smile; no hints
of the psychosis I could smell
in his cologne.

Most days, it doesn't even
feel like gnawing at a bone
that has long been empty.

Unsolicited Advice on How to Love Your Husband: Granny.

men yearn to be
needed by the trophies
they have conquered.

You, baby, are no white flag.

even if you tried to be lace
doily perched on kitchen counter
for him, dry rotting
until you blended with the
walls. there will be no taming

when so much of me is
in your blood. you do know the women
in this family are not the
marrying kind, don't you?

understand that a person who is only
accustomed to surviving will never
know how to live
without eternally looking
for the next thing
determined to kill them.

And I'm sure that man
really loves you, baby.
He probably believes you
are one late night conversation
away from erasing the chalk
outline surrounding your vulnerability,
probably believes you do not
see him as assassin
or thief or a man.

But one day, he will
disapprove of the way you
wear your independence
with all the brazen arrogance
of a suburban police officer with an
itching trigger finger.

he will not understand that you
adore him more than everything but the
broken levy of your pride;
you are willing to let it kill you

still. stay with him until your name
is a rusty iron hatchet in the corner
of his cheek and he stops reaching
for you at night. go to sleep an hour early
to pretend you do not notice
that he no longer comes to bed
with you at all.

when he cheats, take it like a
woman. know he needed something
soft to hide his flaws in; there is
only so much love you can make to
an iron gate hiding rotting flesh.

when he leaves, do not
crumble. remember
your birthright.
cut your hair. buy
new purses. travel.
tell yourself you are not running
away. tell your children you need
"me time". No need to tell the women
you inherited your spine
from anything at all.

Dig a ditch in your insides.
shovel your affection for him
in the same hollow you are hiding
your vulnerability in. Do not
expect it to really die. leave his
tombstone unmarked.

--Brittany Rogers

**

Black Male Anger At *Scandal*: The Real Deal
By Reena Walker

Shonda Rhimes was a single black mother of an adopted child who made it her determination to be number one on TV. She created *Grey's Anatomy*, *Private Practice* and now *Scandal*. She is one of the few black women who can get a project made at a major television network. She has given lots of work to black people and featured them in all sorts of non-traditional roles in her shows and not once have you seen a black man wearing a dress in any of her productions. She doesn't resort to the minstrel stuff and her characters are complex. I doubt very seriously that anyone who has watched *Scandal* would say that the character of Olivia Pope isn't complex and unique. If all you can see is the color of who she is sleeping with on the show and his political party then you aren't watching nor are you looking at the show's character development.

I really think it is wholly unfair the way black men are coming down on this show without really knowing what is going on with this character or looking at their own track record. It is in actuality being taken as a slap in the face to those black men, who more often than not refer to black women as "our women," not because they are tremendously concerned about the well-being of black women and the damage that negative images of black women cause. Rather, they are mostly upset because Olivia Pope's character is independent, has her own desires and career, and makes her own choices. She runs her own firm and is not beholden to any man, and most importantly, is in charge of and controls her own sexuality. She is not a black woman they can own or claim, and this upsets the antiquated notions these men have of black women as property.

Anyone who watches the show knows that the president is actually the one who is obsessed with her and was willing to give up the presidency just to be with her because he loves her and he can't stand his wife. They also know that the president and his wife are going through the motions for the public and have never really been in love. The story line and Olivia's character are varied and complex, so these men really aren't even watching nor are they informed if they are drawing such narrow conclusions.

It is beyond disingenuous for any black man to be upset about this show yet totally disregard his own behavior. The contrast in doing so while being deafeningly silent about the rampant amount of videos, films, music videos, pornography, magazines, comedic routines, You Tube videos, internet memes, radio shows, rap lyrics and theatrical productions that black men have scripted, conceived, created, produced, distributed, promoted and starred in is glaringly hypocritical. The content advocates violence against black women and is demeaning, degrading, objectifying, hyper-sexualizing, stereotyping and dramatizing of black women in a horrendous light and is, to say the least, unseemly. The physical, psychological, emotional and social damage to black women as a result of these images is incalculable.

The vast majority of black men have not stood up in the fight against this sexist onslaught and now are standing in protest of *Scandal* only because they aren't the ones who are in charge of the production and a black man or men is not in control of Olivia Pope's character or her character's sexuality. A black woman is. It is therefore unreasonable and unfair for black men to stand in opposition unless and until they take a pronounced and principled stance against the rampant misogynistic and destructive media content black men have been producing for at least the last thirty years and are just as vocal about it. Nor can they speak about genocide or anything else in that realm when it comes to black women and choice, as they are not, for the most part, adopting the black children that are already here - as Shonda Rhimes did. Until they take action in these areas, they really don't have a leg to stand on when it comes to critiquing this show or any conversation about it.

**

Award-winning (*Lambda Literary Award, Astraea Foundation Poetry Prize Judge, Georgia Author of the Year Award, Chicago Literary Award, Urban Media Maker Award*) poet, performer, playwright, spiritualist, philanthropist, publisher, powerhouse, author, **Robin G. White** skillfully wears many artistic hats. The 40-year pioneer veteran of the arts and activism community has made her niche in ground-breaking erotic stage and screen performances since the late 70s and with her books, *Resurrection: A Collection of Work, First Breath*, and *Reflections of a Life Well Spent,* her plays, "PantyLiners," and "Snatches," her neo-soul, spoken-word band, Sweet Black Molasses and with the trailblazing black, lesbian, ensemble Drag Kings, Sluts and Goddesses.

Deemed "Whitmanesque" by the American Library Association, intelligent, provocative and unrepentant, White's words titillate, invigorate and scintillate, while soulfully and sensually contorting audience emotions, bodies and intellect. Her sexy wit, profound wisdom, and mesmerizing deep vibrato keep listeners squirming at the edges of very moist seats. Her currently available books are *First Breath* and *Reflections of A Life Well Spent*, and look for her children's work under R. L. Young coming soon from GLM Books.

FRIENDS: NNAMDI OKONKWO
[Inspired by the work of artist Nnamdi Okonkwo]

I saw them
Three friends
Of monumental proportions
A testimony to mothers and sisters
Everywhere
Bronzed beauties
With large thighs
And strong legs
Huge arms
And big feet
Sassy and beautiful
In all their full loveliness
And thought
Those are my sisters
No buxomed beauties
No full-figures
No voluptuousness
No caricatured image
Or overly eroticized notion
Just fleshiness
Thickness
Roundness
Plushness
Spread on the bottom
Sagging on the top
Soft in the middle
Womaness
The kind which
Nuzzles warmth
And musk
In its folds

The kind that heats up
Winter nights
When blankets alone
Won't do

The kind that caresses
A child's hurts
And a friend's fears
And yes, the kind
Which yields easily
To a lover's touch
And opens to reveal
A heart which beats
With tenderness and care
And challenges
A notion of what is beautiful.
I saw them three
Friends unabashedly
Chillin' smiling
Relaxing, hanging
Loving
Each other
Like they love themselves
Full
Whole
Beautiful.
And thought,
Yes!
Finally.
Someone gets me!

THE DUSTING

I shuffle, curiously wavering between determined child and flabbergasted
  adult
As I listen for the death-knell ring of raindrops dying
Into dusty crystalline confectionery creations
Beyond my bedroom window.

Brown face pressed, the adult momentarily suspends all childhood magic
To question the sensibility of the neighbor boy's brazen bare arms
Before being once again overtaken by the nine-year old dwelling within
  me.
It is midweek and school days have long since passed
Long pants under plaid school uniforms skirts.
I am safely ensconced in my home in the South
Where the echo of flaccid drops
Splatter in puddles and navigate rivers along every conceivable surface.
The nine year old pouts as it studies the sounds
Hoping for changing patterns or the occasional plink of ice on pavement.
It doesn't come.
I'm a New Englander, born and bred in that bastion of revolution, Boston.
Hard as I try, and as often as my body belies me, I am weathered for these
  storms.
I secretly bemoan the fact that we have all but shut down the city for this
When back home my compatriots march children through eight-foot
  mounds
Onward to their educational destinations with full bags in tow.
On the bus. In the cold. In the snow. Mountains of it.
I watch, praying for just the careless flake to fall.
Mining memories stored like calendars to the body
I march, blue quilted boots over blue quilted pants
Along treacherous mountains
Friend and foe alike hurl bodies across ice
On saucers sharp enough to amputate,
Rust-trailing sleds carry giddy passengers
Along man-made toboggan runs that empty helter skelter
The laughing bounty in a heap.
I long for those memories to be born again,
Long for that innocent equality born of a love for all things winter white.
The hearty New Englander, brown-skin against gleaming white snow
I am the child outside of the Currier and Ives frame,
Beyond the children sledding downhill,
Just behind the trees at the ponds edge, wedging feet into hockey skates,
It is my arm hurling that last lofty snowball against the ice fort.
You can't see me, but I am there.
I am there in a world that denied my existence,
Obliterated the memory of me

Whitewashed the snow, the blood, the rusty red trails.
Dust it over to deny its inelegance. The racism.
But I was there.
And I am here, tonight. Deep in the South.
Waiting with the patience of a nine year old,
For the unlikely snowfall.
The raindrops have stopped falling.
I listen for the quiet hush of an impartial snow
It is a great equalizer.
Please, my nine-year-old heart whispers as I rise
Praying with her for just a dusting.

[*From* ROOTED, *due 2016 from Sunset Pointe Press*]

--*Robin G. White*

**

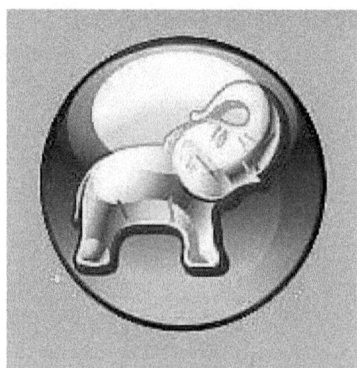